GRAPHIC SCIENCE

THE SHOCKING WORLD OF
ELECTRICITY

WITH MAX AXIOM
SUPER SCIENTIST

by Liam O'Donnell
illustrated by Richard Dominguez
and Charles Barnett III

Consultant:
Dr. Ronald Browne
Associate Professor of Elementary Education
Minnesota State University, Mankato

Capstone
press

Mankato, Minnesota

Graphic Library is published by Capstone Press,
151 Good Counsel Drive, P.O. Box 669, Mankato, Minnesota 56002.
www.capstonepress.com

1 2 3 4 5 6 12 11 10 09 08 07

Library of Congress Cataloging-in-Publication Data
O'Donnell, Liam, 1970–
    The shocking world of electricity with Max Axiom, super scientist / by Liam O'Donnell;
illustrated by Richard Dominguez and Charles Barnett III.
        p. cm.—(Graphic library. graphic science)
    Includes bibliographical references and index.
    ISBN-13: 978-0-7368-6835-8 (hardcover)
    ISBN-10: 0-7368-6835-6 (harcover)
    ISBN-13: 978-0-7368-7888-3 (softcover pbk.)
    ISBN-10: 0-7368-7888-2 (softcover pbk.)
    1. Electricity—Juvenile literature. 2. Adventure stories—Juvenile literature. I. Title.
II. Series.
QC527.2.O44 2007
537—dc22   2006029237

Summary: In graphic novel format, follows the adventures of Max Axiom as he explains the
science behind electricity.

Art Director and Designer
Bob Lentz

Colorists
Ben Hunzeker and Kim Brown

Cover Artist
Tod Smith

Editor
Donald Lemke

TABLE OF CONTENTS

⚡ ENERGY SOURCES

Renewable energy is a source that cannot be used up completely. Water in rivers or the heat from the sun are renewable energy sources. Energy from coal and oil can be used up. They are examples of **nonrenewable energy**.

Energy resources are transformed into electricity at power plants.

Denise is an operator at this coal-fired power plant, where coal is burned to make electricity.

That's right, Max! Nearly a million and a half tons of coal travel up this conveyor belt each year.

Come on. I'll show you where all this material is headed.

MAX AXIOM

TURBINE: Steam from boiling water turns the blades on this machine.

MAGNET: The turbine spins a giant magnet, causing electrons to jump from their atoms.

SUBJECT:
POWER PLANT
GENERATOR

WIRE COIL: Jumping electrons are captured and pushed along a coiled wire.

ELECTRIC FLOW: The charged electrons flow out of the generator as electricity.

Thanks for the tour, Denise. I'm headed to the roof to see where the electricity is going next.

Anytime, Max! Take this walkie-talkie, and give me a call if you need anything else.

13

Wind turbines create power in much the same way. Instead of steam, blowing wind turns the turbine.

Fast moving water can turn turbines as well.

Once the electricity is created, it has to travel from the generator to our homes.

That's why we've come to the roof.

Electricity travels very far, very fast. It flows from the power plant to our homes in a split second.

It doesn't start working until it reaches a looped circuit like the one connecting a lamp.

KLIK

But how does the current make the bulb light up?

Inside the bulb is a metal called tungsten. It can carry an electric current but not as much as the copper wire.

Tungsten is called a resistor. It blocks some of the electric current. The blocked current turns into energy.

RESISTOR

ELECTRICITY

In 1752, inventor Benjamin Franklin flew a kite during a thunderstorm to prove that lightning is electricity. As his kite entered a darkened cloud, electricity surged down the string to a key Franklin had attached to the end. When Franklin touched the key, he got a shock. This painful experiment convinced Franklin that lightning and electricity were the same.

In fact, lightning is an extreme form of static electricity. Inside storm clouds, small particles rub together to create a negative electrical charge. This negative electricity stretches down toward positive electricity, which begins rising from the ground. The opposite charges meet to form a brilliant bolt of lightning.

On October 21, 1879, inventor Thomas Edison created an incandescent light bulb. Nearly three years later, he opened the first central power plant in New York City. Soon, thousands of Americans were lighting their homes with Edison's bulbs.

Storms are filled with natural electricity, but sunny skies have energy as well. Solar power is a renewable source of energy from the sun. Specially designed panels called cells capture sunlight and turn it into electricity.

The wires that carry electricity to our homes are extremely dangerous. So, how do birds perch safely on top of them? Electricity always looks for the closest path to the ground. Since birds aren't touching the ground, electricity continues safely along the wires. However, if a person touches the wires while in contact with the ground, he or she could receive a deadly electric shock.

Electricity can also be generated through nuclear fusion. During this process, atoms are smashed together to create an extra electron. The electron creates energy to boil water and turn a turbine. Like solar power, nuclear energy doesn't pollute the air. Unfortunately, it creates dangerous waste.

Creating electricity often creates pollution, which can be harmful to the environment. To help reduce the amount of electricity used in your home, replace at least one incandescent light bulb with a fluorescent bulb. They can last almost 13 times longer and save electricity. If every U.S. household switched just one bulb, the amount of pollution prevented would compare to taking 1 million cars off the road.

MORE ABOUT

SUPER SCIENTIST

Real name: Maxwell J. Axiom
Hometown: Seattle, Washington
Height: 6' 1"   Weight: 192 lbs
Eyes: Brown   Hair: None

Super capabilities: Super intelligence; able to shrink to the size of an atom; sunglasses give x-ray vision; lab coat allows for travel through time and space.

Origin: Since birth, Max Axiom seemed destined for greatness. His mother, a marine biologist, taught her son about the mysteries of the sea. His father, a nuclear physicist and volunteer park ranger, schooled Max on the wonders of earth and sky.

One day on a wilderness hike, a megacharged lightning bolt struck Max with blinding fury. When he awoke, Max discovered a newfound energy and set out to learn as much about science as possible. He traveled the globe earning degrees in every aspect of the field. Upon his return, he was ready to share his knowledge and new identity with the world. He had become Max Axiom, Super Scientist.

Glossary

amp (AMP)—a unit used to measure the strength of an electrical current

circuit (SUR-kit)—a path for electricity to flow through

conductor (kuhn-DUHK-tur)—a material that lets electricity travel easily through it

current (KUR-uhnt)—a flow of electric charge

electrons (i-LEK-tron)—a tiny particle in an atom that travels around the nucleus

energy (EN-ur-jee)—the ability to move things or do work

generator (JEN-uh-ray-tur)—a machine that makes electricity by turning a magnet inside a coil of wire

insulator (IN-suh-late-ur)—a material that blocks an electrical current

nucleus (NYOO-klee-uhss)—the center of an atom; a nucleus is made up of neutrons and protons.

proton (PRO-tahn)—one of the very small parts in an atom's nucleus

turbine (TUR-bine)—an engine powered by steam or gas; the steam or gas moves through the blades of a fanlike device and makes it turn.

watt (WOT)—a unit for measuring electrical power

READ MORE

Binns, Tristan Boyer. *A Bright Idea: Conserving Energy.* You Can Save the Planet. Chicago: Heinemann, 2005.

Richardson, Adele. *Electricity: A Question and Answer Book.* Fact Finders. Mankato, Minn.: Capstone Press, 2006.

Saunders, Nigel, and Steven Chapman. *Renewable Energy.* Energy Essentials. Chicago: Raintree, 2006.

Stille, Darlene R. *Electricity.* Science Around Us. Chanhassen, Minn.: Child's World, 2005.

Walker, Sally M. *Electricity.* Early Bird Energy. Minneapolis: Lerner, 2006.

INTERNET SITES

FactHound offers a safe, fun way to find Internet sites related to this book. All of the sites on FactHound have been researched by our staff.

Here's how:
1. Visit *www.facthound.com*
2. Choose your grade level.
3. Type in this book ID **0736868356** for age-appropriate sites. You may also browse subjects by clicking on letters, or by clicking on pictures and words.
4. Click on the **Fetch It** button.

FactHound will fetch the best sites for you!

INDEX